Sports Illustrated
SAFE DRIVING

The Sports Illustrated Library

BOOKS ON TEAM SPORTS

Baseball	Curling: Techniques and Strategy	Ice Hockey
Basketball	Football: Defense	Soccer
	Football: Offense	Volleyball

BOOKS ON INDIVIDUAL SPORTS

Badminton	Horseback Riding	Table Tennis
Fly Fishing	Skiing	Tennis
Golf	Squash	Track and Field: Running Events

BOOKS ON WATER SPORTS

Powerboating
Skin Diving and Snorkeling
Small Boat Sailing
Swimming and Diving

SPECIAL BOOKS

Dog Training   Training with Weights
Safe Driving

Sports Illustrated
SAFE DRIVING

By CHRIS PACKARD

Illustrations
By Chuck Queener

J. B. LIPPINCOTT COMPANY
Philadelphia and New York

U.S. Library of Congress Cataloging in Publication Data

> Packard, Chris.
> Sports illustrated safe driving.
>
> (The Sports illustrated library)
> 1. Automobile driving. 2. Automobiles–Safety measures. 3. Traffic safety. I. Title.
> TL152.52.P3   629.28'3'2   73–12153
> ISBN–0–397–00991–7
> ISBN–0–397–00992–5 (pbk.)

Copyright © 1974 Time Inc.
All rights reserved
Printed in the United States of America

Cover photograph: John Lamm
Photograph on page 8: Mercedes-Benz Corporation.
Photographs on pages 12, 26, 60, 75 and 79: General Motors Corporation.
Photograph on page 17: UPI.
Photographs on pages 23, 37, 48, 80–83 and 85: John Lamm.
Photographs on pages 32 and 33: Chrysler Corporation Engineering.

The author appreciates the assistance and materials supplied him by American Safety Equipment Corporation, Firestone Tire and Rubber Company, Mercedes-Benz of North America and the staff of the General Motors Proving Ground.

Contents

INTRODUCTION	9
1. THE VEHICLE	15
FRONT-ENGINE, REAR-WHEEL DRIVE	18
FRONT-ENGINE, FRONT-WHEEL DRIVE	19
REAR-ENGINE, REAR-WHEEL DRIVE	20
MID-ENGINE	21
OPTIONAL EQUIPMENT	22
DISC BRAKES	22
POWER BRAKES	24
POWER STEERING	25
LIMITED-SLIP DIFFERENTIAL	27
HEAVY-DUTY EQUIPMENT	27
FEDERALLY REQUIRED SAFETY EQUIPMENT	28
PRECRASH	30
POSTCRASH	31
CRASH	31
2. TIRES	35
BIAS-PLY TIRE	40

Radial-Ply Tire	41
Belted-Bias-Ply Tire	43
Tire Maintenance	45

3. VEHICLE DYNAMICS 49
Braking	51
Steering	53
Rear-Wheel Lockup	54
Cornering	57
Understeer	58
Oversteer	59
Skidding	61
Spin Out	64

4. ADVERSE CONDITIONS 65
Winter Driving	65
Off-Road Recovery	71
Tire Blowouts	74
Loss of Brakes	74
Staying Awake	76

5. THE ACCIDENT 77
The Potential Accident	78
The Accident Situation	84
The Accident	88
The Postaccident	93
The Safe Driver	94

Sports Illustrated
SAFE DRIVING

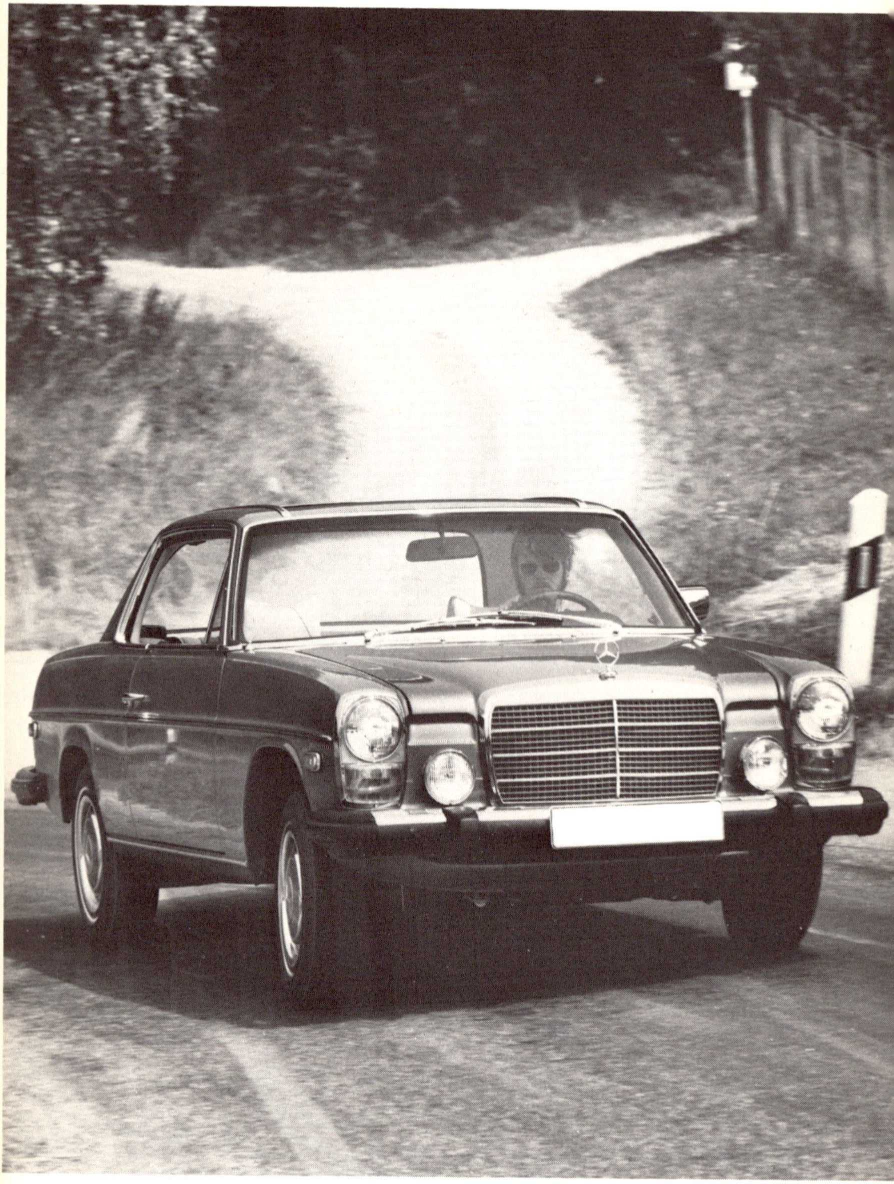

Introduction

STATISTICALLY, each of us will be involved in an auto accident about once every three years. How we drivers react to an emergency—whether we freeze up, slam on the brakes and slide out of control, or attempt to evade the accident entirely—is directly related to our ability to perceive the cause of accidents before they happen.

All of driving is an integrated system of the driver, the vehicle and the driving environment (the road, weather conditions, daylight, etc.) and to be understood it must be approached as a total unit. As a nation concerned with death on the highway, we have always been vaguely aware of the interdependence of the three elements of driving, but it was not until a few years ago, when William Haddon, Jr. was appointed administrator of the National Highway Safety Bureau (a division of the Federal Department of Transportation), that we began taking a logical, integrated approach to highway safety.

Haddon was given the task of creating a national program

to reduce death and injury on America's highways, and one of his first acts was to draw up a simple matrix (see Diagram 1) that reduces all the factors in road deaths and injuries to nine simple categories.

Haddon's matrix was adopted by the Federal Department of Transportation as the organizing principle for all its highway safety programs. There is at least one Transportation Department safety standard corresponding to each of the

	DRIVER	VEHICLE	ROAD AND ENVIRONMENT
PRE-CRASH	1	2	3
CRASH	4	5	6
POST-CRASH	7	8	9

Diagram 1. Haddon's matrix.

nine boxes of the matrix, and in some cases, Box 5, for example, there are more than a dozen federal safety standards that apply.

Since 1968, the safety of the automobile has improved dramatically. Auto manufacturers have been installing enough federally required safety equipment in every car to

> Box 1. Driver in a precrash situation: driver-education programs, alcohol-control programs, improved licensing procedures.
>
> Box 2. Vehicle in a precrash situation: improved braking systems, federal tire tests, instrumentation and visibility standards.
>
> Box 3. Road in a precrash situation: improved roadside lighting, easily read road signs and route numbering, clearly defined lane and road-edge demarcation.
>
> Box 4. Driver in a crash situation: same as Box 1.
>
> Box 5. Vehicle in a crash situation: collapsible steering columns, padded dashboards, seat belts, headrests, impact-absorbing side-body and door structures.
>
> Box 6. Road in a crash situation: guardrails, breakaway lamp poles and road signs, bridge abutments moved far back from the road's edge.
>
> Box 7. Driver in a postcrash situation: same as Box 1.
>
> Box 8. Vehicle in a postcrash situation: strengthened fuel tanks and fuel lines that maintain their integrity under the stress of an impact, nonflammable materials in the car's interior.
>
> Box 9. Road in a postcrash situation: government-supported ambulance purchases, ambulance-crew training, roadside-emergency telephones, improved rescue equipment, wide, paved breakdown lanes.

During evasive driving drills at a driver-education course, students are instructed to avoid panic breaking.

better the inhabitant's chances of accident survival by as much as 100 percent over models built before 1968. And in recent years, roads and highways have become safer. State and federal highway departments have worked together to do such things as moving bridge abutments and other roadside "boobytraps" back, away from the edge of our roads, and guardrails now separate the opposing sides of most divided highways, vastly reducing the possibility of head-on collisions.

These improvements are all necessary and, when they exist in sufficient numbers, will go a long way toward saving lives. But, the driver is still the problem in the government's safety programs. He cannot be legislated as easily as steel and concrete, and because he can think and make decisions, his actions cannot be predicted and controlled by a safety standard.

So, very little of our national highway safety effort is devoted to teaching the driver how to avoid trouble on the road, or, if he does find himself in an accident situation, how to escape with a minimum of human and property damage. Unfortunately, most of our driver-education courses seem to operate on the theory that if a student can learn to drive well enough to get his driver's license, he can probably drive well enough to stay out of accidents.

Safe Driving was written to fill this void. It is a survival handbook, written for the driver from the driver's point of view, and covers, in varying degrees, the nine boxes in Haddon's matrix—but always from the perspective of the individual motorist and his relationship to his car and the driving environment. It assumes that each of us will be confronted with potential accidents every day, and it attempts to supply the average driver with the training he needs to identify and escape these situations.

The reader need not have an extensive knowledge of automobiles to use the information in this book, nor is there anything in the following pages that requires special equipment or the facilities of an auto-racing track. The driving techniques are all common sense, and the vehicle-control exercises can all be self-taught in a supermarket parking lot on a Sunday afternoon; then many can be practiced while driving to and from work or school—when most accidents occur.

1
The Vehicle

THE AUTOMOBILE BUSINESS IN AMERICA has grown to be the biggest and richest in the world by catering to the individualist in each of us. We are led to believe that no matter how bizarre our tastes or eccentric our precise demands, we can order the car we want. The real problem, of course, is figuring out what we want.

There are so many different makes, models, sizes, colors, optional extras and design philosophies available that the buyer is often overwhelmed by the choices. However, if you could study these choices, you would discover that, besides the obvious differences in the color, styling and the selection of optional equipment, the cars are fundamentally all quite similar.

Since all manufacturers offer approximately the same range of colors and optional equipment, there are really only two basic elements which make cars organically different from one another—the size of the package and the arrangement of the drive-train components. But these two basic elements are critical to any driver's mental attitude toward driving. For example, a rear-engine, rear-wheel-drive car may satisfy all a motorist's requirements for packaging efficiency, winter traction and ease of repair (see drive-train descriptions below), but if he cannot adjust to the car's handling characteristics, he will never be a safe driver. In a potential accident situation, he will falter for an indecisive moment, and that hesitation may be just enough to keep him from avoiding the accident.

Many people buy bigger cars than they need because they believe a large car offers them better protection in an accident than a small car. To some extent they are correct. When a big car and a small car meet in a direct head-on collision, the small one receives more damage than the big one. However, the flaw in this line of reasoning is that the direct head-on collision seldom occurs. The driver of one of the vehicles usually maneuvers out of the collision course before the impact. And small cars are considerably more maneuverable than big cars.

The big-car-versus-small-car controversy often boils down to the car buyer's feelings about the role of fate in an accident. Owners of the big models are likely to believe that when the time comes, an auto accident is almost inevitable. And many small-car owners refuse to believe that they are predestined to become involved in accidents, feeling their own driving ability and their car's maneuverability will allow them to avoid accidents.

But whether a car is big or small, locating the engine and transmission in the front, rear or middle of the car, or driving the car by its front wheels rather than its rear wheels, are not decisions made arbitrarily by an auto manufacturer. Each design has strong advantages and disadvantages that must be weighed against one another before a manufacturing decision is made. The car buyer must weigh the same advantages and disadvantages before he spends his money.

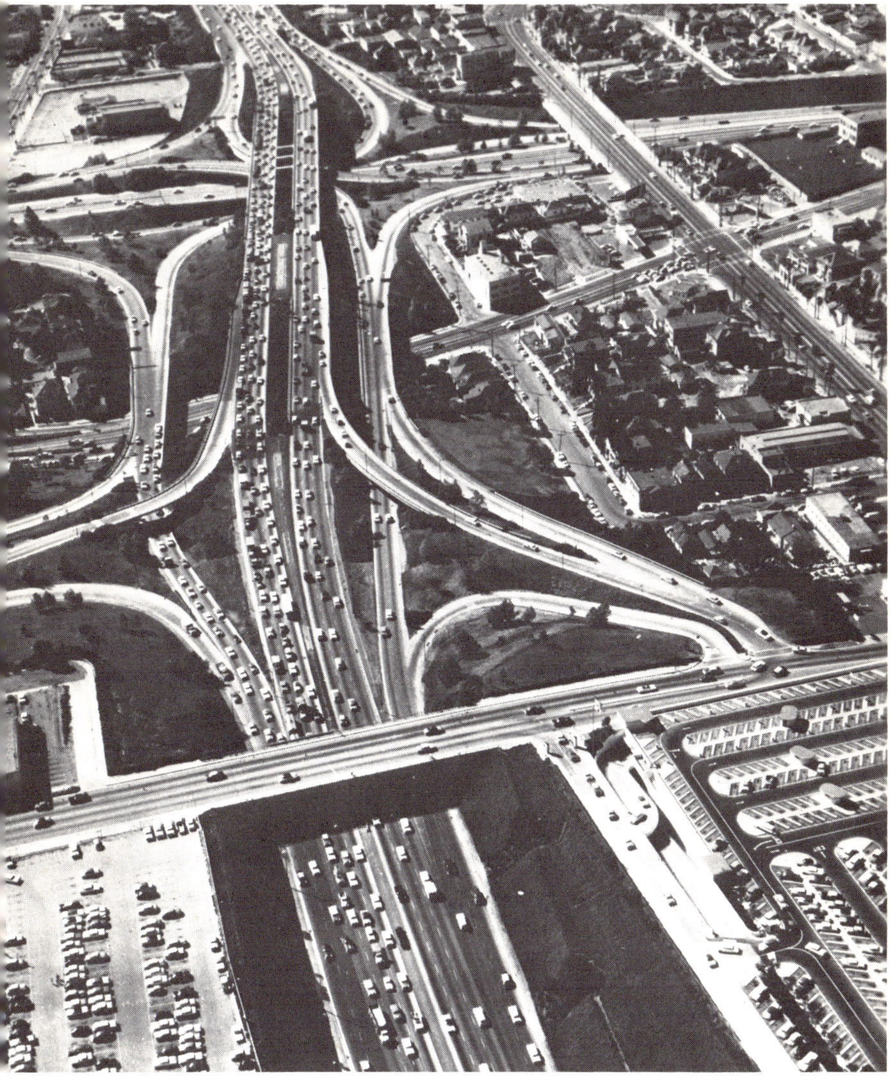

FRONT-ENGINE, REAR-WHEEL DRIVE

The majority of the world's cars use a front-engine, rear-drive layout because it is quite cheap to manufacture, allows moderate luggage space in the rear, separates the drive-train components for easy repair or replacement and sets the large mass of engine between the driver and any object he hits in a frontal impact.

On the other hand, the front-engine, rear-drive arrangement uses interior space for the drive-shaft and transmission tunnel (the hump running down the center of a car's floor), and because the engine weight is at the opposite end of the auto from the drive wheels, the front-engine, rear-drive car has the worst traction characteristics of any design. The engine weight in front also causes the car to understeer in corners (see Diagram 9 and explanation on page 58).

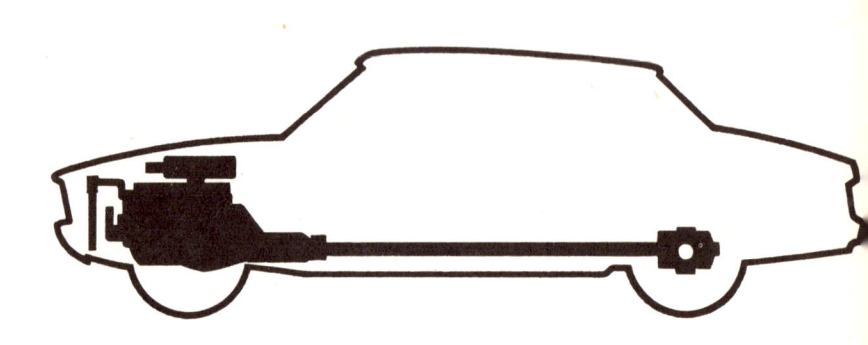

Diagram 2. Front-engine, rear-wheel drive.

FRONT-ENGINE, FRONT-WHEEL DRIVE

An increasing number of the world's auto makers believe it is more efficient to pull a car along the road by its front wheels than to push it by the rear wheels, and they are finding the production process is simplified because the total front-drive power unit (engine, transmission and differential) is installed as a single piece.

With the entire propulsion mechanism bolted on out front, auto-body design becomes an exercise in creating the most efficient shape for housing people and their luggage

Diagram 3. Front-engine, front-wheel drive.

without having to accommodate a transmission and driveshaft hump along the car's backbone.

Front-wheel-drive cars are more expensive to manufacture than the more conventional front-engine, rear-drive models because the drive shafts, that transfer power from the engine to the front wheels, must also act as the steering system, involving a series of complex designs and intricate machining processes to operate effectively.

So, front-wheel-drive cars have amazing traction because the engine's weight is directly over the drive wheels, but generally require more steering-wheel effort to turn a corner because the drive and steering mechanisms must both be manipulated with every steering input. Front-wheel-drive cars display pronounced understeer when cornering.

REAR-ENGINE, REAR-WHEEL DRIVE

Although similar to the front-drive system because the drive train is manufactured as a unit, then bolted on the back of the passenger compartment, the rear-engine, rear-drive car is cheaper to manufacture because the drive is through the rear wheels and the steering through the front wheels, eliminating hours of costly machining. Also, like front-wheel drive, the engine weight is over the drive wheels for superior traction.

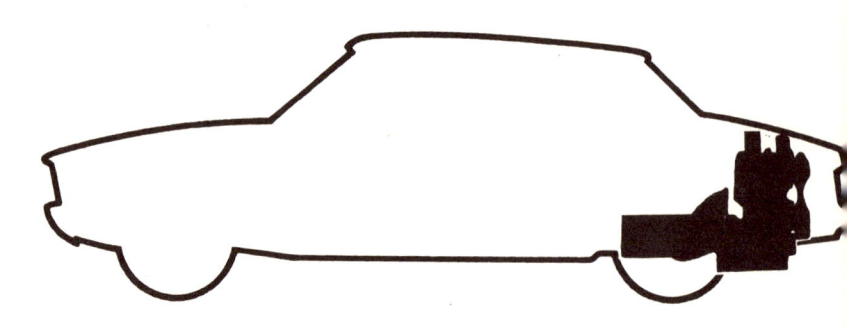

Diagram 4. Rear-engine, rear-wheel drive.

Because the gas tank, front suspension and steering mechanism must be housed in front, the rear-drive car tends to have minimal luggage space, often an irregular-shaped pit between the front wheel wells. Unlike the automobiles most American drivers are used to, the rear-engine, rear-drive car has strong oversteer tendencies when cornering (see Diagram 10 and explanation of oversteer on page 59).

MID-ENGINE

Used in only a few two-seat models and in many of the world's racing cars, a mid-engine layout would be impractical if not impossible to carry out in a sedan because, to be effective, the engine must be located in the middle of the car, just behind the driver's head. The transmission bolts on behind the engine, with the differential in the same housing and the drive shafts sticking out the sides, leaving little space in the rear for luggage. Like the rear-drive car, there isn't much luggage capacity in the front, either.

What the mid-engine car does have going for it is handling. With the engine mounted low, at almost exactly the middle of the structure, a mid-engine car is capable of generating amazingly high cornering forces with neutral handling characteristics. This means that where the front-engine car gives in to the pull of centrifugal force at the front and heavier end first (understeer), and the rear-engine car succumbs to centrifugal force at the rear wheels first (oversteer), the mid-engine car, in theory, breaks loose with all four wheels at the same time. It drifts sideways toward the outside of the corner—a technique most race drivers favor for fast, safe cornering.

Diagram 5.   Mid-engine.

Regardless of where the engine and drive wheels are located in any auto you are buying, there will undoubtedly be optional equipment to contend with. In this case, the new-car buyer, although he represents less than 10 percent of the total car population of the United States, is the most important car owner. His choices in the automotive marketplace this year directly affect what the rest of us, the nation's used-car owners and buyers, will have to choose from a few years hence.

We cannot advise how automobiles should look; that is a very personal matter. And we cannot define a convenience because one man's convenience is another man's annoyance. We can, however, suggest some optional equipment that will make driving safer and more enjoyable.

OPTIONAL EQUIPMENT

Disc Brakes

For more than half a century all the world's cars were stopped by drum brakes, and it wasn't until the 1960's that the aircraft-type disc brake first saw extensive use on automobiles. Most manufacturers now offer disc brakes as standard or optional equipment on the front wheels only. Drum brakes are retained in the rear because it is cheaper to incorporate a parking brake in a drum than a disc.

A drum brake stops a car by expanding two stationary shoes against the inside of a spinning drum that is attached to the wheel. To understand how a drum stops your car, put your loosely tightened fist into a can or mailing tube slightly larger than your fist. Using your other hand to rotate the tube, try to stop the rotation by expanding your fist. You'll find your fist, that is simulating the operation of the brake shoes, does not do a very effective job stopping the tube.

With his car in a violent skid, this driver properly corrects the situation by turning the front wheels in the direction of the skid.

The disc-brake system uses a stationary caliper that squeezes against a spinning disc fastened to the wheel. Its action can be approximated by taking your fist out of the tube and using the thumb and fingers of the same hand to grasp the wall of the tubing. Now, try to rotate the tube with the other hand. You'll find your hands are more effective as a disc brake (squeezing) than as a drum brake (expanding).

Disc brakes are also much more resistant to fading after long, repeated application in a short time period than drum brakes. The disc brake is open to the air flowing under the car and uses that air for cooling. Because the drum brake is an enclosed system, most of the heat generated in hard braking is trapped within the drum, and this causes fading to set in quite rapidly. A loss of the car's braking ability results.

To understand the heat generated during braking, rub the palm of your hand rapidly back and forth on your pants leg. Before long, the friction of your rubbing will generate so much heat you will have to take your hand away. In this exercise, if you were working hard, you may have generated as much as 20 foot-pounds of energy in either direction.

The average car traveling 20 mph is generating about 40,000 foot-pounds of forward energy; at 40 mph, the force quadruples to 160,000 foot-pounds of energy. When you remember how hot your hand got just generating 20 foot-pounds of energy against your pants, you can easily understand why the brake-lining material in drum brakes turns from a solid state to a liquid and gaseous state when the brakes are used repeatedly in a short period of time, as in descending a mountain.

Power Brakes

Specifying the power-brake option when you order a new car doesn't get you larger-diameter drums, more lining surface or wider discs than the standard manual brakes. What you do get is a vacuum-actuated booster between the brake pedal and the hydraulic braking system. It's the mechanical equivalent of being fitted with a leg two or three times stronger than your normal leg.

Early power-brake systems seemed to have only two positions—full on or full off. They were so sensitive, any extra pressure on the brake pedal would bring the car to a lurching, skidding stop with all four wheels locked up.

In recent years, power-braking systems have improved considerably. They have become more linear, coordinating the brake-pedal travel with increased braking capacity. In other words, the harder or further you push the pedal, the more stopping power you summon. You get the feel and control of a manual brake without having to exert the extremely high brake-pedal pressure required to stop a heavy, modern car with manual brakes. And since you don't have to concentrate all that human energy on the brake pedal, you have energy left to steer your way out of an accident situation.

Power Steering

Like power brakes, power steering has been vastly improved in recent years to the point where the most modern systems provide much of the "feedback" or "road feel" of manual steering without the effort. This hasn't always been so. Many early versions of power steering transferred so little feeling of the road back through the steering wheel that the drivers of cars equipped with these systems often got themselves into trouble—the first warning of an icy or slippery road is a sudden "light feeling" in the steering; if your car's steering feels light all the time, you do not get the message about the road conditions until too late, if at all.

Another point in favor of power steering is that, like power brakes, the effort needed to use the system in an emergency is not so great that you are off-balance or have no strength left for corrective measures.

High-speed off-road recoveries are practiced at advanced driver-training programs.

Still, if you do not need power steering, there is little sense paying for it. Before buying a new car, try test-driving similar demonstrators with and without power steering. If you are considering a compact- or subcompact-size auto, or a small import, you may find you are able to drive and park without benefit of a power assist on the steering. Besides, even the best power-steering system provides the driver with less "road feel" and costs more to repair than a manual system.

Limited-Slip Differential

If you live in a snowbelt area or do much driving on unpaved roads, you should consider this option (less than $100) offered by many manufacturers. A normal differential distributes the engine's power to the drive wheels separately, along the path of least resistance. In the winter, a car having one drive wheel on ice and the other on dry pavement may not be able to move under its own power. The wheel on ice, offering less resistance, spins freely while the wheel on the pavement refuses to turn.

With a limited-slip differential, the internal mechanism chooses the drive wheel with the best traction and distributes power to it, denying power to the wheel without traction. In a slippery driving situation, like a snow-covered road, the limited-slip differential will continually shunt back and forth between the drive wheels, altering the application of power as the conditions change. It works equally well in mud and sand.

Heavy-Duty Equipment

A decade ago, an optional heavy-duty suspension package would endow the average unladen passenger sedan with a ride like a pickup truck, jarring the driver's teeth the first time a mildly bumpy section of road was encountered. But, as in many other facets of our daily lives, the computer has changed all that.

The modern computer-designed standard suspension has noticeably improved the ride and handling properties of the passenger car. The computer-designed optional suspension system produces in even the largest sedans what feels like sports-car handling and cornering, with none of the harshness and choppiness associated with pickup trucks. But, even this comparison is no longer valid because the modern pickup has benefited greatly from computer-designed suspension.

Heavy-duty suspension is most highly recommended. With its superior handling, cornering and road-holding abilities, it is obviously an asset to safe driving, but few buyers specify it on their options list. This may be because many manufacturers hide it, calling it a trailer-towing package or a rally kit.

Heavy-duty cooling systems, clutches, brakes (usually finned rear-drum brakes to dissipate heat faster), axles, seats, carpets and sometimes even engines and transmissions can often be found on a manufacturer's list of special equipment for police cars and taxicabs.

If your local dealer seems reluctant to order the heavy-duty equipment you want, try another dealer and be persistent. Remember, auto manufacturers and dealers are in business to sell cars and if you want special equipment badly enough, you'll find a dealer willing to order it for you. Besides, heavy-duty options (HD-suspension costs less than $50 from many manufacturers) are among the best values for the automotive dollar.

FEDERALLY REQUIRED SAFETY EQUIPMENT

Purely from the standpoint of safety, the best value for the automotive dollar is a car built to the federal government's safety standards. Under the National Traffic and

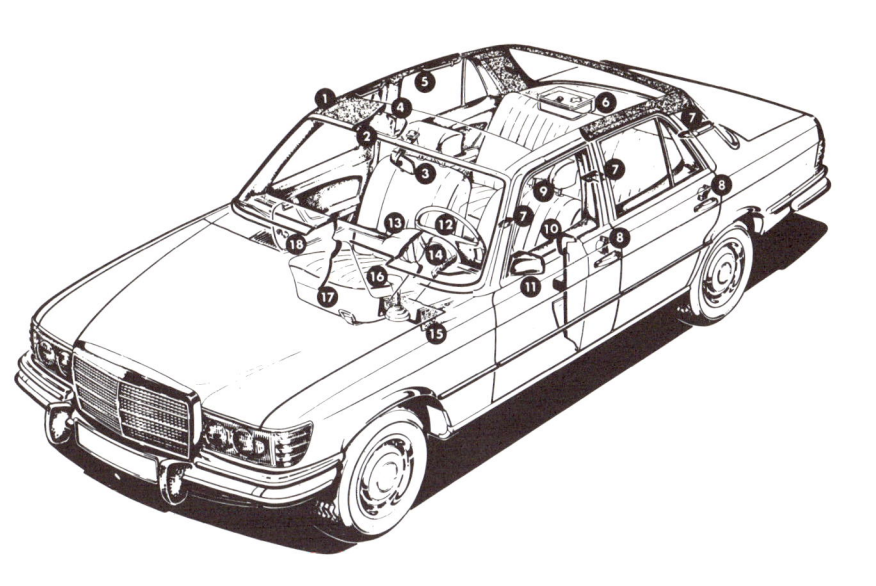

Diagram 6.   Safety equipment.
1. Roof frame padded all the way round.
2. Recessed and padded sun visors.
3. Antidazzle rear-view mirror that breaks off on impact.
4. Three-point safety belt, recessed with inertia reel.
5. Flexible handles.
6. First-aid box recessed.
7. Door pillars padded.
8. Child-proof safety locks on rear doors, and measures to stop the doors bursting open in the event of an accident.
9. Head rests.
10. Padded doors and arm rests.
11. Antidazzle wing mirror, adjustable from the inside, folds back if struck as measure to protect pedestrians.
12. Steering wheel with padded rim and hub.
13. Nonreflective instruments set into dashboard, and operating elements which yield on impact.
14. Impact absorber and collapsible telescopic steering column.
15. Console and oddments tray yielding on impact.
16. Padded gear lever.
17. Knee protection.
18. Door handles are flush-fitted.

Motor Vehicle Safety Act of 1966, the federal Department of Transportation established minimal safety-performance standards for all automobiles manufactured after December 31, 1967, for sale in the United States. Each year since, more standards were added and those already in force improved. Cars manufactured since December 31, 1969, incorporate all of the following required features (listed according to their intent):

Precrash

(1) A hood-latch and safety-catch system to prevent accidental opening.

(2) Dual-circuit braking, incorporating a secondary circuit should the main hydraulic circuit fail, a warning light to indicate a failure in the hydraulic system and improved hydraulic-brake hoses.

(3) A parking brake capable of holding the car on a 30 percent grade.

(4) The standardization of the automatic transmission-shift indicator, with a neutral position between the park and reverse positions and the ignition switch wired to prevent starting the car in anything but the park or neutral positions.

(5) An outside rear-view mirror on the driver's side of the car.

(6) Two-speed windshield wipers, a windshield washer and a defroster and defogger on the inside of the windshield. Wiper, headlight and ignition switches must be clearly labeled and within reach of drivers wearing seat belts.

(7) Bright metal within the driver's view (windshield-wiper arms, hood ornaments and other trim) must be manufactured or coated in a way that reduces glare.

(8) Backup lights, side-marker lights on front and rear fenders and front and rear hazard-warning flashers are re-

quired. Cars with concealed headlights must be designed to prevent the compartments from closing while the lights are in use.

Postcrash

An improved fuel system and fuel tank to reduce the chance of fuel spillage and fire in an accident.

Crash

(1) An energy-absorbing steering column that collapses or cushions the driver in a crash rather than spearing him through the chest.

(2) Head restraints at the top of the two outside front seats to protect the driver and passenger from "whiplash" and other neck injuries.

(3) A specially laminated windshield that, in a crash, reduces head and face cuts and acts as a safety net, keeping occupants from being thrown out of the car.

(4) Padding on the instrument panel, sun visors, armrests and front-seat backs.

(5) Door latches and hinges designed to prevent opening under impact, protecting the occupants from being thrown out of the car.

(6) Lap-type seat belts in all passenger positions with upper torso (shoulder belts) in the two outside front-seat positions.

After December 31, 1971, a warning light and buzzer were required to remind the occupants to buckle their belts, and after August 15, 1973, an ignition-switch interlock was required, making it impossible to start the engine until the driver and the right-front-seat passenger buckled their seat belts. When this book was written, the federal government

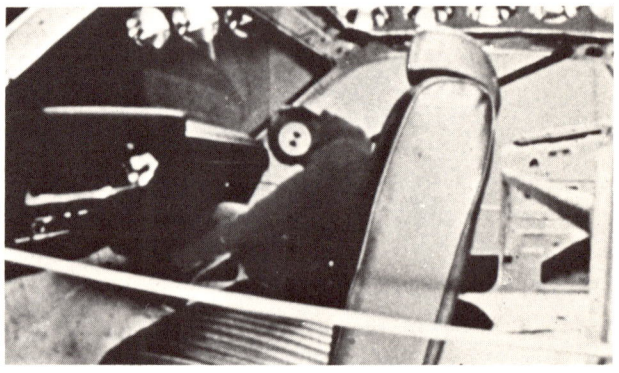

Illustration 1A. Driver wearing shoulder/lap belt is restrained on impact.

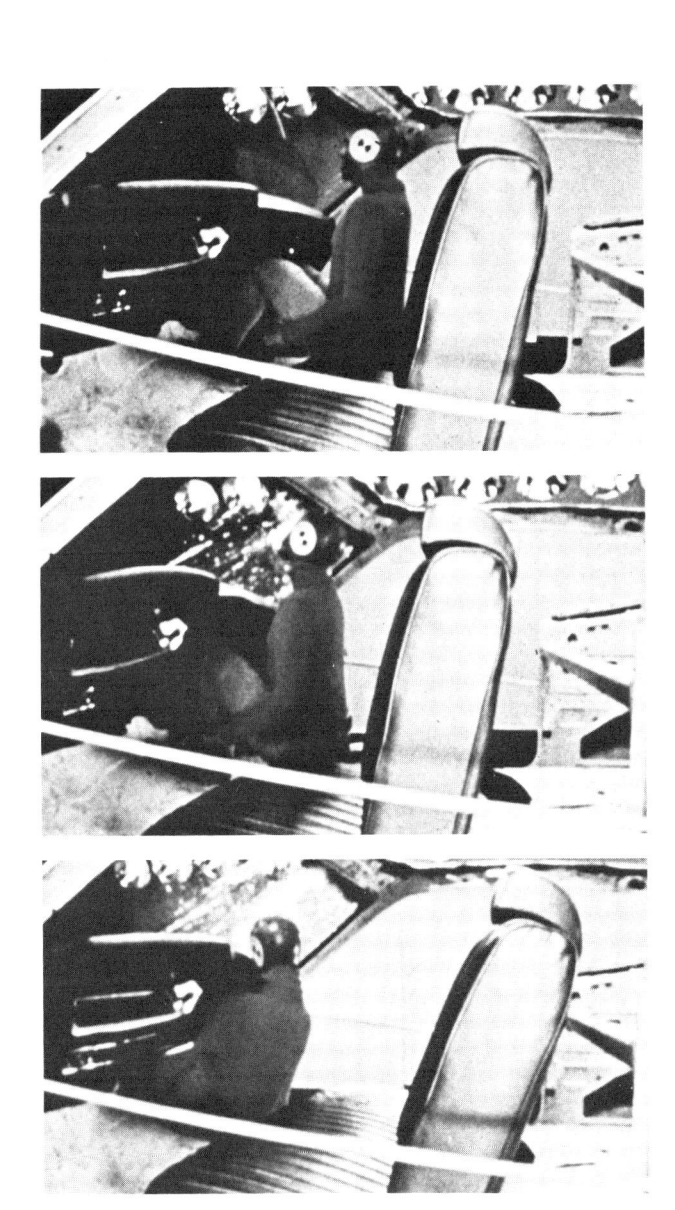

Illustration 1B. Driver not wearing shoulder/lap belt is thrown against windshield on impact.

and auto manufacturers were still debating the feasibility of fully passive restraint systems (air belts, air bags, nets, etc.) that would protect a car's occupants in case of an accident but not require the occupants to take an active role in their own protection. Buckling a seat belt is thought by the government to be an active role.

Regardless of the government and industry arguments over the definitions of active and passive, lap/shoulder seat belts factory-installed in every car for sale in the United States after December 31, 1967, are the single most important life-saving device available.

A Swedish study of nearly 30,000 auto accidents showed that not one of the almost 10,000 occupants wearing lap/shoulder belts was killed in crashes at speeds up to 60 mph. A General Motors Engineering Center study of 230 accidents in which the occupants were wearing either lap or lap/shoulder belts uncovered only two fatalities among lap/shoulder-belt users. Yet, in both studies unbelted occupants were killed at speeds less than 20 mph when they were either thrown out of the car or received fatal injuries striking the car's interior with great force.

If the statistical evidence of these two studies doesn't convince you to buckle your lap/shoulder belt before you even turn your car's ignition switch (regardless of whether your destination is 5 miles or 2,000 miles away), then look at the visual evidence in Illustration 1.

Lap belts should be snug and worn low, across the pelvis, not across the stomach where, in a severe impact, they might cause internal injuries. Shoulder belts should be tightened to leave just enough slack to allow the width of a fist between the driver's chest and the belt. Any more slack can reduce the shoulder-belt's ability to protect the occupant because, as you can see in the illustrations, the shoulder belt will stretch under the severe stress of an impact. For this reason, lap and shoulder belts worn in an accident should be immediately replaced. They can only stretch once, so they can only save your life once. But, once should be enough.

2
Tires

WHEN NEWSPAPERS PUBLISH accident reports stating that "The driver was injured when he lost control of his car, skidding off the road into a tree," they're printing a rough approximation of the circumstances, not an accurate record of the events. A driver *does not* lose control of his car, but he frequently allows his auto's tires to lose their grip on the road. The result is often the same—an accident—but the distinction is important.

No matter what a driver does behind the wheel—steering, accelerating or braking—his message is carried out by his car's tires. And they are the car's *only* link with the road. A vehicle can run head on into a bridge abutment only if the front tires steer that path; two automobiles collide on a snowy road because one driver tried to brake too hard, allowing the tires to slide on the slippery surface; and a car can only fishtail when accelerating if its tires are permitted to lose positive contact with the road surface.

Compared to the familiar movement of the human body,

the automobile has comparatively little contact with the ground. To understand this difference clearly, take a tracing of your car's "footprint"—the same thing you do if ordering shoes for yourself through the mail.

Lay a large sheet of paper on the driveway and slowly drive your car's front tire onto the paper. With a pencil or ballpoint pen, trace around that part of the tire that is contacting the paper, then back the car off the paper. Now place your shoe next to the tire's outline on the paper and trace your own "footprint."

In comparing the two tracings, you'll probably be amazed to discover the car's "footprint" is not significantly larger than your own. And even if you consider that the car's total "tread-patch" area (sum of all four tires' contact area) is significantly larger than your own total "tread patch" (sum of the contact surface of both feet), the car still comes out second best in a comparison of potential traction.

A car is ten to thirty times as heavy as you are, can travel at a top speed five to seven times as fast, cruises effortlessly at a speed four times as great as your fastest running speed and is capable of generating steering, braking and lateral acceleration (cornering) forces up to and exceeding the force of gravity, yet has little more than twice the area of contact with the ground that you have.

When you lose your footing on a slippery floor or icy sidewalk (roughly equivalent to a car losing its grip on the road) and you fall to the ground, the impact is often enough to hurt you, or shake you up. But the fall has little more than the force of your own weight behind it. When you imagine the severity of the fall a 4000-pound car takes if it loses its footing, you begin to understand the importance of a driver never allowing his vehicle to lose its grip on the road.

Automobile tires, like shoes, are not all the same. An expensive leather dress shoe is more comfortable to many people than a tennis sneaker, but you would hardly wear a

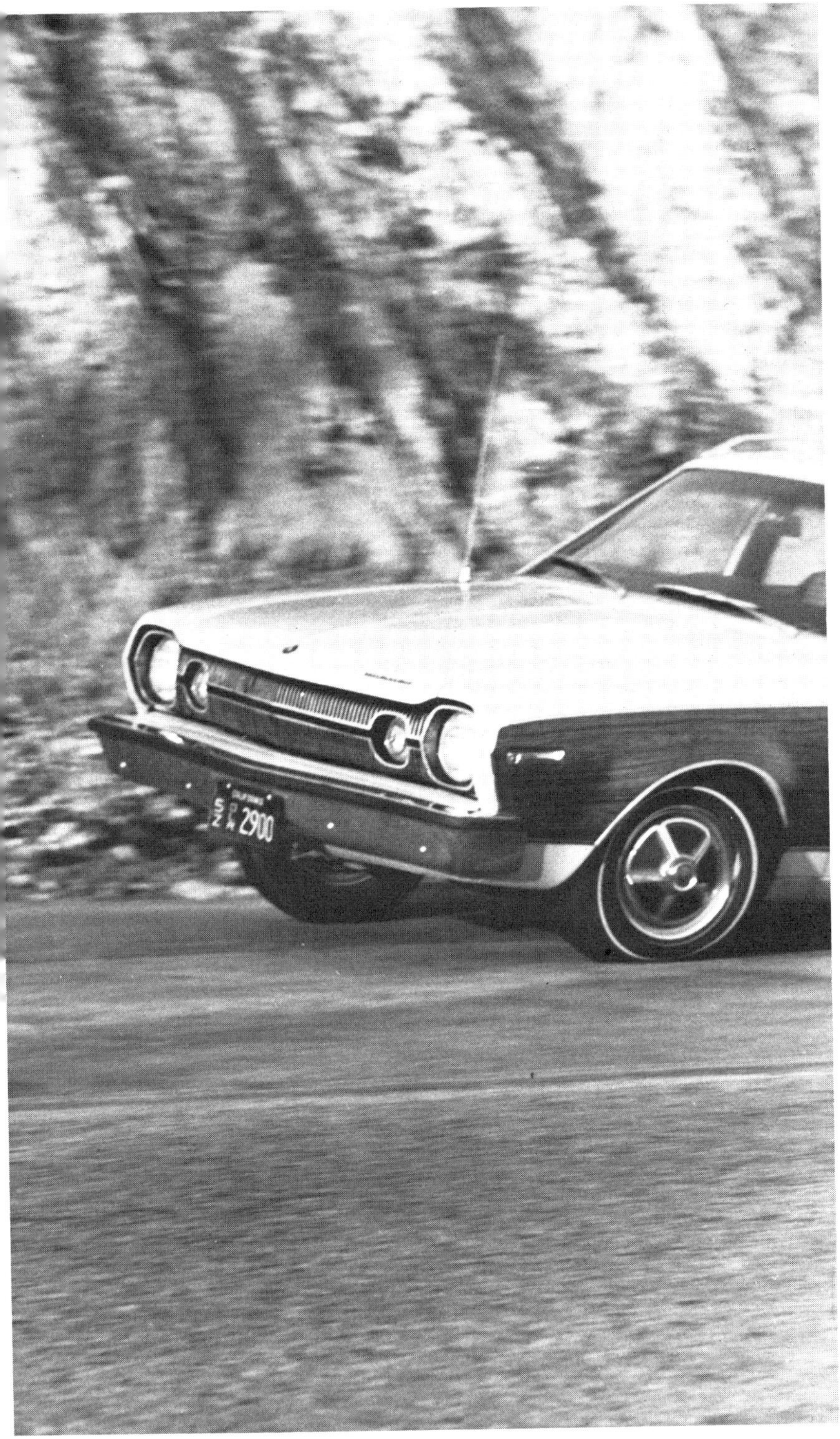

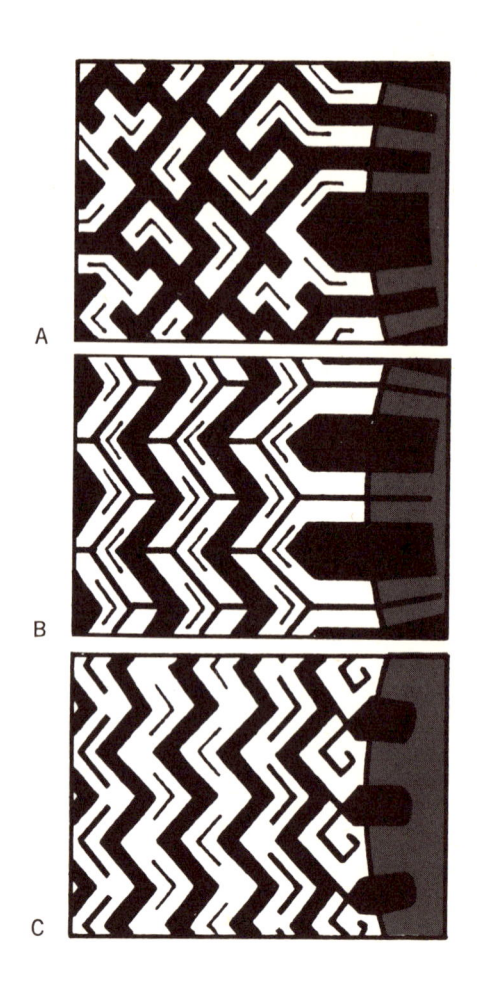

Diagram 7. Not all snow tires are the same; different areas need different tread patterns. The rural outback, annually inundated with well over 100 inches of snow, requires (A) a large, open-lugged tread. Areas bordering on the snowbelt need (B) a tread that combines lugs for snow and drainage channels for rain. Suburban areas with efficient snow-removal equipment need (C) a pattern with modified lugs to plow through the morning's snow, and maximum rubber on the road to provide the best traction on the afternoon's dry pavement.

dress shoe on the tennis court. Nor would you wear sneakers to a formal dance. Because different shoes satisfy different requirements, many of us buy two or three different pairs and often a pair of boots for wet weather.

Unfortunately, it is not so easy to change a car's tires as it is to change shoes. During the winter, many car owners living in snowbelt areas exchange the conventional drive-wheel tires for snow tires, but even this change is more of a compromise than the perfect match of traction to road conditions one might imagine.

During a blizzard, a car needs the grip of tire chains to make headway, and a few hours later, when the plows uncover the pavement, the same car needs conventional tires for maximum traction. Since car owners are not willing to install or remove tire chains every few hours, the snow tire is used. It has neither the traction of chains nor the dry-pavement grip of a conventional tire, but it will do both jobs adequately.

Although the snow tire is the most obvious example, all tires represent some type of compromise on the part of the tire manufacturer. Because tire manufacturing is still largely based on the skilled hands of production-line workers, the more complex a tire, the more it costs. And the more properties a manufacturer tries to design into a tire, the more complex it becomes.

However, the tire manufacturer is not the only one who compromises. You, the ultimate consumer in the tire-manufacturing and sales process, must also make some compromises when spending your money. There is no one tire that combines the best of ride, handling and wear characteristics. The closer you try to come to this ultimate, the more it costs. So, in the end, you decide which characteristics (including price) are most important and choose accordingly.

Although there are almost as many different tread patterns as tires on the market, it is not the tread that makes the real difference between tires. It is the construction of the tire carcass (the main body of the tire, hidden beneath the tread) that determines a tire's ride, performance and price. There are three methods of carcass construction in widespread use today—(1) bias ply, (2) radial ply and (3) belted-bias ply.

BIAS-PLY TIRE

Ever since the tire industry first put an inner tube and air instead of hard rubber inside tires, tire carcasses have been constructed with alternating layers of crisscrossing fabric.

Like a piece of plywood, that is also constructed in layers with the grain of each layer crossing the preceding layer at right angles, the bias-ply tire is strong and rigid. But as in plywood, the bias-ply tire has little ability to flex because the opposing grains of succeeding layers work against each other, causing friction and eventually heat—the major cause of tire failure and short tread life.

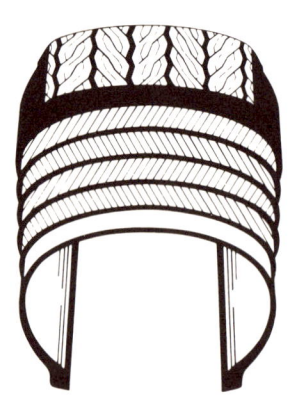

Diagram 8A.
Bias-ply tire.

Despite its drawbacks, the bias-ply tire does have the advantage of being the cheapest tire available, costing little more than half the price of a comparable belted-bias tire or a third the price of many radials. And for the budget-conscious car owner who seldom drives more than 50 mph and never subjects his car to severe cornering, braking or acceleration loads (all causes of rapid heat buildup in tires), it may be the best buy.

RADIAL-PLY TIRE

The significant difference between the radial-ply tire and the bias-ply tire is the radial's ability to flex at the sidewall. This eliminates much of the friction and heat generated within the tire's carcass, resulting in what seems like phenomenal tire life—three to four times the wear of a set of bias-ply tires mounted on the same car.

Diagram 8B.
Radial-ply tire.

Sidewall flex is also the reason radial tires vastly improve the braking and cornering ability of any car they are mounted on. To understand why this is, stand with a chair a foot or two away from your left hand and plant your right foot firmly on the floor.

Now, keeping your right foot flat on the floor, lean your body to the left as far as you can, using the chair for balance. You will find that, because your ankle flexes, you can lean quite far to the left without your shoe's sole lifting from the floor.

If you repeat this exercise, but concentrate on keeping your ankle rigid, you will lift the right edge of your shoe sole off the floor almost as soon as you start leaning. This is the way a bias-ply tire acts under high cornering forces.

Like the rigid-ankle exercise, the auto-body lean lifts the outside edge of the inside tires, reducing their grip on the road surface so the car eventually gives in to the centrifugal forces on it and slides toward the outside of the corner.

The radial tire is able to sustain much higher cornering forces because its sidewall flexes (like your ankle), allowing the car body to lean while keeping the tire's tread flat on the road surface.

When a car is steering or braking, the tire's shape tends to distort under the forces imposed on it. A radial tire takes these forces in stride; absorbing the distortion in its flexible sidewall, but the bias-ply tire's rigid structure cannot easily accommodate this movement. So, the distortion is played out in the bias-ply tire's tread section, causing the tread to squirm on the road surface. This reduces the effectiveness of the braking and the precision of steering and imposes unnecessary wear on the tire tread.

The radial tire's rigid tread and flexible sidewall are, at the same time, its greatest asset and its outstanding deficiency. Because the radial tire's tread is intentionally rigid (the purpose of the circumferential belts under the tread), the slightest bump in the road is transferred directly to the car's body and eventually to the passenger's body. The bias tire's unreinforced tread is capable of more give and bounce and will therefore absorb the millions of small pavement imperfections it encounters in every mile of driving.

So, if you are convinced that the radial tire's superior cornering, steering, braking and tread life are worth the extra money the tire costs, be prepared to live with a noticeably harsher ride.

BELTED-BIAS-PLY TIRE

The belted-bias-ply tire is the in-between tire. It does not have the handling, braking or tread life of a radial-ply tire, yet does all these things better than a bias-ply tire. It is not as cheap as the bias-ply tire and not as expensive as the radial.

The belted-bias-ply tire has a bias-ply-type carcass constructed of thin, flexible fabric to approximate the radial's

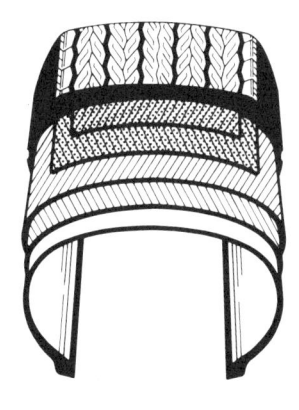

Diagram 8C.
Belted-bias-ply tire.

sidewall properties, but it is "laid up" on much the same machinery as the bias-ply tire to keep costs down.

Fiberglass or polyester belts are wrapped around the tire's circumference beneath the tread to approach the radial tire's strength and rigidity. The resulting tire wears longer than a bias-ply tire but not as long as a radial. Its ride qualities, cornering ability and braking effectiveness are also about midway between the cheapest and most expensive tire.

Caution

Tire types must not be mixed on any car. If your car is equipped with bias-ply tires and you decide to replace them with radial-ply tires, radial-ply tires must be mounted on all

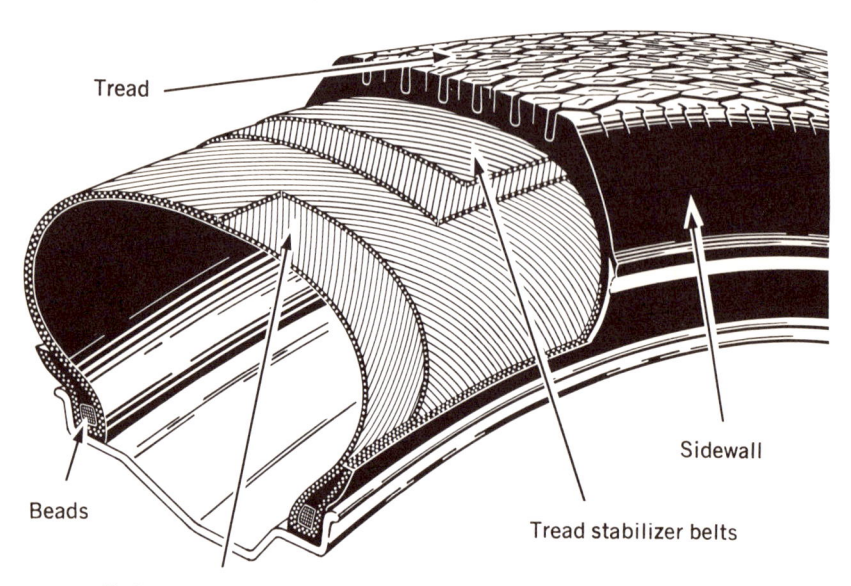

Diagram 8D.
ANATOMY OF A BELTED-BIAS-PLY TIRE.

four wheels. The same is also true of belted-bias-ply tires.

Each type, and often each specific brand, of tire relates to the road surface with its own peculiar pattern of squirms and oscillations. When a car's four tires are all the same, these movements tend to work in concert, canceling each other out. If there is a mixture of dissimilar tires on a car, the minute tire movements will act against each other, causing the car to dart from side to side of the road as well as being the cause of a variety of seemingly unexplainable twists, wiggles and shakes in the front suspension and steering.

TIRE MAINTENANCE

No matter what type or brand of tire is mounted on your car, you can improve tire safety, mileage and performance with just ten minutes of maintenance a week.

Make it a habit once a week to get down on your hands and knees to look at your car's tires. Check for worn spots, irregular wear and the warning signs of future suspension problems.

You can also check the tire's tread depth without fancy equipment, using nothing more than a Lincoln-head penny. Push Abe Lincoln's head into the grooves between the ridges of tread. If you can see the top of his head in any of the grooves, the tread is too worn for safe driving.

If only the outside edges of the tread are worn, the tire has been used without enough air in it (underinflation). Too much air (overinflation) will cause premature wear to the center of the tread only. Both conditions can be avoided by keeping your car's tires inflated to the proper pressure at all times.

Tire pressure should be checked once a week and only when the tires are cold (the car shouldn't have been driven more than a few miles after an overnight rest). Do not trust

Properly inflated tire shows even wear across tread.

Underinflation causes excessive wear at edges of tread.

Overinflation causes excessive wear in center of tread.

Illustration 2.

the gauge on the air hose at the corner service station. A National Bureau of Standards survey showed these gauges may be misreading by as much as 12 pounds. Instead, buy yourself a tire-pressure gauge at an auto-parts or accessory store and keep it in your car's glove compartment.

The correct tire pressure, as indicated in your car-owner's manual, was calculated by the manufacturer of your car to provide the best combination of ride, handling and tire life. There is, however, an exception to this rule. If you are pulling a trailer or carrying an exceptionally heavy load in the luggage compartment, you should increase the pressure in the rear tires by 3 to 5 pounds per square inch. This should be done only when the tires are cold; in no case should the pressure exceed the maximum cold-inflation rating established by the Federal Department of Transportation and displayed in raised letters on the tire's sidewall.

Remember, one of the major causes of tire failure is internal heat buildup, which results primarily from too little air pressure in the tire. So, check tire pressures once a week to maintain your car's performance and prevent dangerous internal damage to the tires. Your tires will also benefit from longer tread life.

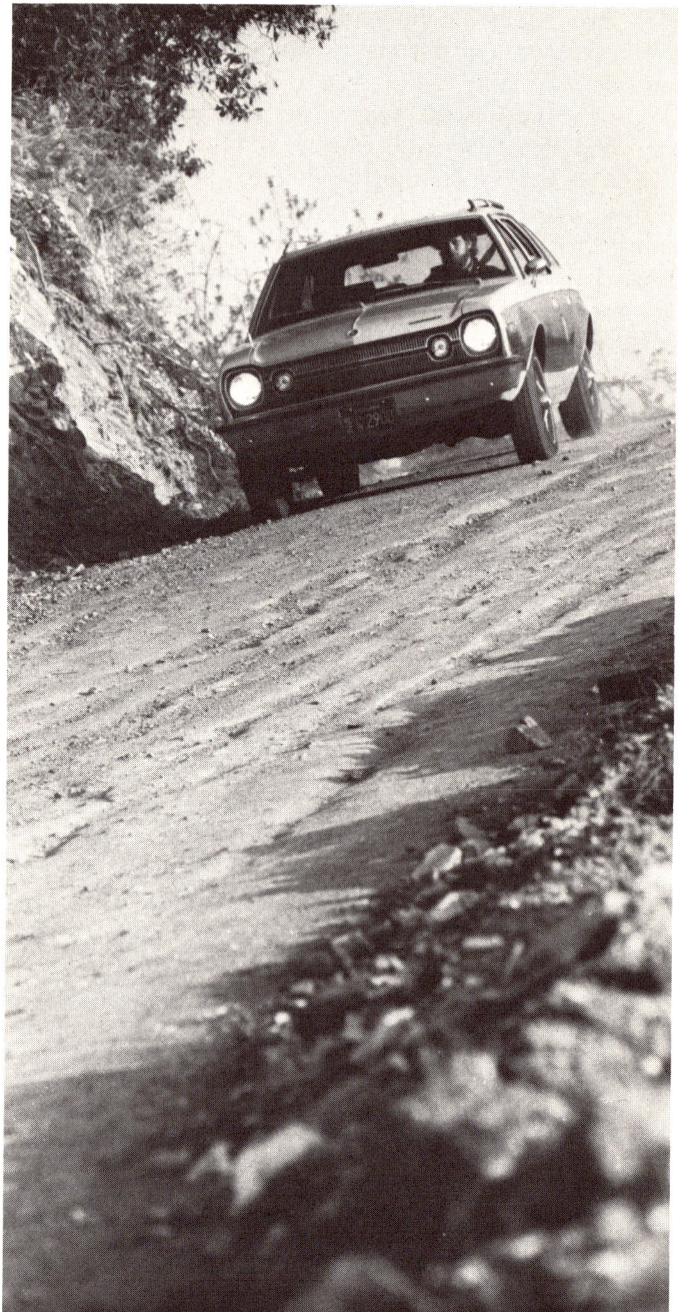

3
Vehicle Dynamics

LEND AN UNFAMILIAR DINGHY to an experienced small-boat sailor and he will immediately sail to a secluded area and attempt to capsize the boat. This is not a display of disdain toward the borrowed boat. It is the most rudimentary form of boating safety. Once a sailor knows how far a boat will tip before overturning, he can sail it hard for years without getting into trouble.

The automobile driver, on the other hand, often finds himself in difficulty because he never took the time to learn his car's limits of control. It is not necessary to overturn your car to discover these. Unlike most sailboats, the automobile will slide or skid out of control long before it overturns, but that unmanageable movement is just as dangerous to the automobile driver as capsizing is to the sailor.

The most serious shortcomings in the education of most drivers in this country are they (1) do not have any notion until it is too late that they are losing control, (2) do not know how to correct their loss of control and (3) do not have any idea of the relationship between the elements of control.

Some basic rules of control that every driver should know are:

(1) A tire that is not rotating (as when the brakes are locked up) cannot steer.

(2) A tire that is sliding sideways can neither brake nor steer.

(3) A tire sliding to a stop (brake lockup) has a reduced grip on the road surface, and thus less stopping ability than a tire that rolls to a stop.

(4) A car's rear wheels can have as much effect on steering as its front wheels.

Illustration 3. Although the steering wheel is turned all the way to the driver's right, his car still heads straight ahead because the brakes are locked.

To be a safe driver, you must understand these rules with your head *and* with the seat of your pants. Some of the exercises that follow, such as braking and steering, are merely variations of skills used in everyday driving. Other exercises, like skidding and sliding, are the very situations every driver seeks to avoid in routine driving.

To a driver who has never experienced a skid, the sudden loss of control can be frightening, resulting in a variety of erratic and panicky attempts to wrestle the car under control. The inexperienced driver, in this state of panic, is a hazard both to himself and others on the road.

Skid control, like steering and braking, is a skill to be learned and perfected at the individual driver's pace, outside the confines and pressures of normal traffic. So, find yourself a large, open, unpaved parking lot or a wide gravel road on which to practice.

The main things to look for are seclusion (early Sunday morning is a good time to practice because most people are home sleeping) and a surface with a low-traction coefficient. Dirt, gravel, ice and packed snow are all excellent surfaces because they allow you to duplicate at lower, safer speeds the loss of control you might experience on paved roads.

BRAKING

Traveling at 20–30 mph in a straight line, slam on the brakes. HARD. As you would if a child suddenly jumped in front of you. Under this braking force, all four of your car's wheels will lock up and the tires will slide over the road surface.

Try this exercise a half-dozen times so you will know how sliding feels. Locking up all four wheels on dry pavement at 60 mph feels the same, but doing so at 30 mph on gravel is safer and does not wear the tread off the tires.

Now, begin in the same way again (30 mph, hard on the brakes) but, instead of treating the brake pedal as a lever that must be driven through the floor, think of it as a tennis ball. Don't bang on it; squeeze it with your foot.

When you first feel the car sliding, reduce your squeezing just enough to stop the slide. Then squeeze just that fraction more needed to bring on the slide. And back off again. With practice, you can develop a delicate and accurate touch, allowing the auto's wheels to slide or not as you wish. You will also find that the car stops in a shorter distance when you bring it almost to the point of sliding but no further.

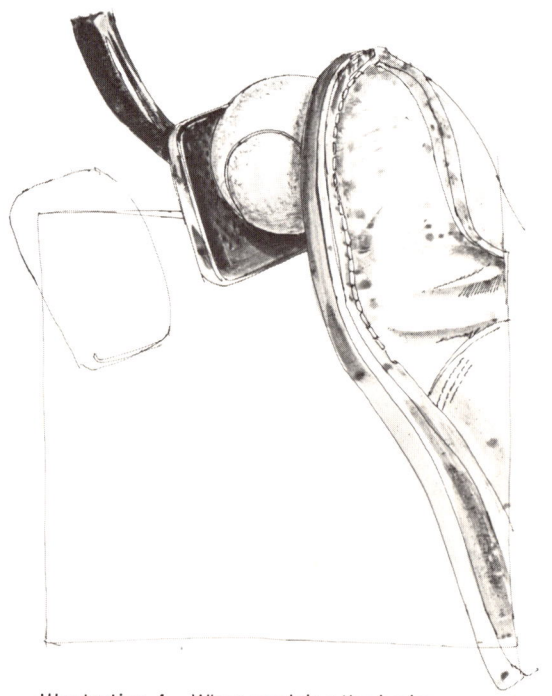

Illustration 4. When applying the brake, the driver squeezes the pedal lightly, as if a tennis ball were under his foot.

STEERING

Now, place an empty cardboard box in the car's path. Approach the box directly at about 30 mph. When you are about 50 feet away, slam on the brakes and try to stop before hitting the box. If you do hit the box, which you probably will, don't worry, it won't harm your car.

A passenger is often helpful in this exercise, particularly if you don't brake until he yells "Brake!" Drawing a bead on the box at 30 mph, you'll wait for the command, and if it doesn't come until you are right on top of the box (30 feet or less), you will probably panic and slam the brakes on hard, causing the car to slide directly into the box.

Try it again, only this time concentrate on braking and steering around the box to the left. If you lock the brakes in panic (it is the passenger's job to try to get you to do this), you can turn the steering wheel as far to the left as you want but the car will continue sliding straight ahead—right into the box. Remember, a tire that is not rotating cannot steer.

Do the exercise again. This time concentrate on squeeze braking and turning the steering wheel. You will find that during the time the brakes are not locked up, the car will follow your movements of the steering wheel. With practice, you will be able to develop a rhythm of squeeze braking and steering, approach the box at 30 mph, hit the brakes 30 feet away, brake and steer a path out of an imaginary right lane, to the left of the box, and back into the right lane, where you will come to a full stop a few feet beyond the box.

Repeat this until you can do the exercise perfectly; it may save your life some day. And every time you have to stop your car, if only for a traffic signal, THINK SQUEEZE BRAKING.

REAR-WHEEL LOCKUP

Some cars, particularly those with large, heavy engines in the front and naturally weak or mushy front springs, may lock up their rear wheels long before their front wheels under hard braking. This happens because most of the car's weight is transferred forward, lightening the load on the rear wheels, allowing them to slide more easily over the road surface.

Illustration 5. Weight transfer during braking.
(A) A car's weight during normal driving is fairly evenly divided between the four wheels.

It is a condition you can live with if all your stopping is in a straight line. But, if you try to steer and brake, as in the previous exercise, the rear end of the vehicle may slide sideways in little hops as the brakes are alternately locked and released. It is a case of a tire that can neither brake nor steer sliding sideways.

If your car's rear-wheel lockup is particularly severe, there are really only two things you can do. (1) Have a competent mechanic install a brake-proportioning valve between

(B) When the driver applies the brakes excessively hard, most of the car's weight is transferred to the front wheels, allowing the lightly loaded rear wheels to skid along the surface of the road without exerting much braking force.

the front and rear brakes to reduce the braking effort at the rear wheels, or (2) install new, stiffer front springs and shock absorbers to resist the weight transfer to the front of the car. This will concentrate more weight on the rear tires and press them into better contact with the road, reducing their tendency to slide over the road surface.

Illustration 6. The rear end of the car slides sideways when the rear wheels are locked up in a hard braking situation.

CORNERING

All cornering is a physical battle between the tires' grip on the road and the centrifugal force bearing on the car, pushing it ever outward from the center of the imaginary circle whose arc the car is scribing. At low speeds, when there is the least centrifugal force, the tires win the battle and the car easily follows the course the driver sets.

As the speed of the car increases, the centrifugal force increases, eventually placing a greater sideways thrust on the car than the tire's grip on the road is able to overcome. The auto then slides sideways, away from the center of the imaginary circle.

You can safely explore these forces on an open parking lot or some other large, unobstructed paved area. With your car in the center of the area, slowly (10 mph) begin driving around in a circle 100–200 feet in diameter. Hold the steering wheel steady on that course and gradually increase your speed.

First, you will be aware that your auto's body is leaning toward the outside of the circle in response to the centrifugal force being exerted on it. Don't worry about the car overturning; at this speed, it is virtually impossible on a smooth surface.

Next, the tires will howl and squeal and possibly smoke a bit as they have to fight for their grip on the road. Then, as your car's speed around the circle increases even more, either the front or rear tires will lose their grip on the pavement and begin sliding toward the outside of the circle. On a 200-foot-diameter circle, this will occur between 25 and 35 mph.

If the front wheels slide first, it is called understeer. If the rear wheels are the first to lose their grip, the condition is called oversteer. You can learn to correct either condition.

UNDERSTEER

An understeering car (usually one with most of its weight on the front wheels) tries to turn a corner into a straight line, leaving the circle front wheels first. The driver must respond by turning the front wheels at an increasingly sharper angle to keep the car following the circle. Finally, the front tires are turned at so great an angle to the car's path that they lose their grip on the road and begin sliding sideways.

To correct understeer, the driver must gently ease up on the accelerator pedal while turning the steering wheel slightly back toward the center position, reducing the tires' turning angle just enough to regain their grip on the road.

These corrections must be made gradually and gently. If the driver suddenly removes his foot from the accelerator

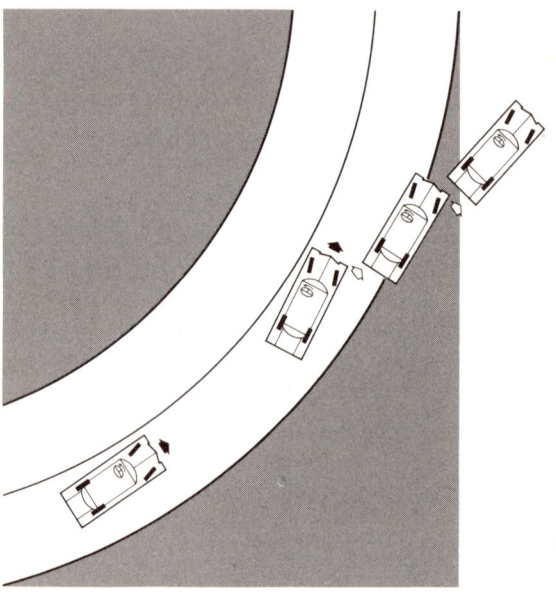

Diagram 9.
Understeer.

pedal rather than just slightly reducing the pressure on the pedal, he may find himself contending with a situation called "trailing-throttle oversteer." This is no more than a sudden change from understeer to oversteer when the power is removed from the drive wheels.

OVERSTEER

An oversteering car's rear wheels lose their grip on the road first, causing the whole rear end of the automobile to swing toward the outside of the road and off the road, rear end first, if uncorrected. To correct oversteer, the driver must reduce the angle at which the front wheels are turned. After lifting your accelerator-pedal foot, merely turning the steering wheel back toward its center position is enough to cure most mild oversteer.

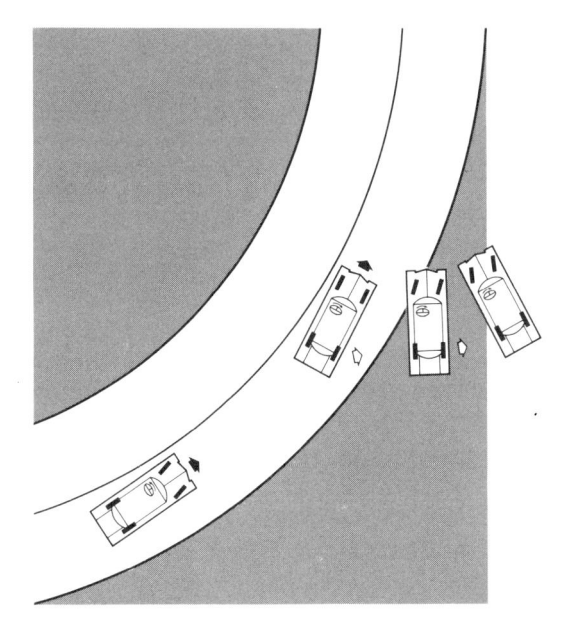

Diagram 10. Oversteer.

On a wet, slippery surface a student driver finds himself out of control because he has jammed on his brakes, locking all four wheels. A much softer "touch" on the brakes is required for these conditions.

Practice correcting oversteer until you can do it well; then practice until it is second nature to you. The amount you turn the steering wheel to correct oversteer is critical—too little will not stop the car's rear end sliding sideways and too much will cause the car to sway in the opposite direction.

Even if you own a car with strong understeering tendencies, it is important that you know how to correct oversteer because a skid is no more than oversteer gone uncorrected. And no car is immune to skidding.

SKIDDING

The first warning most drivers get of a skid is the rather sudden feeling that they are going down the road sideways. Regardless of whether the skid was brought on by a patch of oil in the road or some loose gravel in a corner, the cure is the same—take your foot off the accelerator pedal and steer the car in the direction of the skid. RELAX. Depress the clutch in manual-transmission cars. DO NOT TOUCH THE BRAKE PEDAL. Act decisively, but do not overreact by turning the steering wheel too far, or you will find yourself skidding in the opposite direction.

You can practice skid control on a large, open dirt or gravel area. To induce a skid to the right (rear wheels sliding to the right) at low speed, step down hard on the accelerator to get the rear wheels spinning and yank the steering hard to the left. Or while your car is traveling 20–30 mph, stomp on the brakes hard enough to induce a slide and then steer hard and fast to the left.

Either way, at the moment you feel the skid start, you should begin taking corrective action, steering in the direction in which you want the car to go. In this instance (skidding to the right), you need to bring the car back to the straight-ahead position, so you must turn the steering wheel to the right—in the direction of the skid. As you practice, you may become overeager and set up for yourself a skid situa-

Illustration 7. How *not* to control a skid. (A) and (B) The car begins to turn and slide. (C) and (D) The driver has not turned the steering wheel in the direction he wants the front wheels to go and the car is skidding out of control.

Illustration 8. How to control a skid. (A) The car is beginning to make a 90-degree turn into a side road. (B) The rear end of the car is sliding. (C) The driver brings the front wheels back in the direction he wants the car to go. He is now in control and has stopped the skid. (D) He is back in his original path.

tion that occurs at too high a speed for your abilities or comes on faster than you expect. By the time you start turning the steering wheel to correct the skid, you will realize the car has gone beyond the point at which it can be rescued from the skid and that your car is "spinning out."

SPIN OUT

There is really nothing the driver can do in a "spin out" except sit back, relax and ride it out. It is an utterly helpless feeling. Once your car begins spinning, you can panic, saw back and forth on the steering wheel attempting to correct the spin and try the brake and accelerator, but none of your actions will have much effect.

The best way to ride out a spin is to depress the clutch (manual-transmission cars) or shift to neutral (automatics) and attempt to hold the steering wheel steady, pointing as close to straight ahead as possible. AND RELAX. When the car finally comes to rest in a real-life spin out, you will need your full concentration to move it immediately out of the path of other cars on the road.

By practicing skids and spin outs, you will eventually develop an almost instinctive sense of the skid coming on before it actually happens and react properly out of the same instinct.

4
Adverse Conditions

UNLIKE THE PRIMARY DRIVING SKILLS (steering, speed control and braking) that are used all the time, the techniques needed to deal with adverse driving and weather conditions must be learned, practiced and then stored away in the driver's head until he has occasion to use them.

WINTER DRIVING

Ice and snow are the most slippery road surfaces (short of oil or grease) that any driver is apt to encounter. Chart 1 shows the distance required to stop a car on ice is about five to eight times as great as on dry pavement, depending on the type of tires used. Snow is almost as slippery as ice.

Since it takes so much more road to stop a car traveling on snow or ice, the first rule of winter driving is to allow more distance between your car and those ahead. Greater stopping distance also means that a vehicle will take a greater amount of time to come to rest once the brakes are applied,

BRAKING DISTANCES
FROM 20 MPH

- ON DRY PAVEMENT: 17 FT.

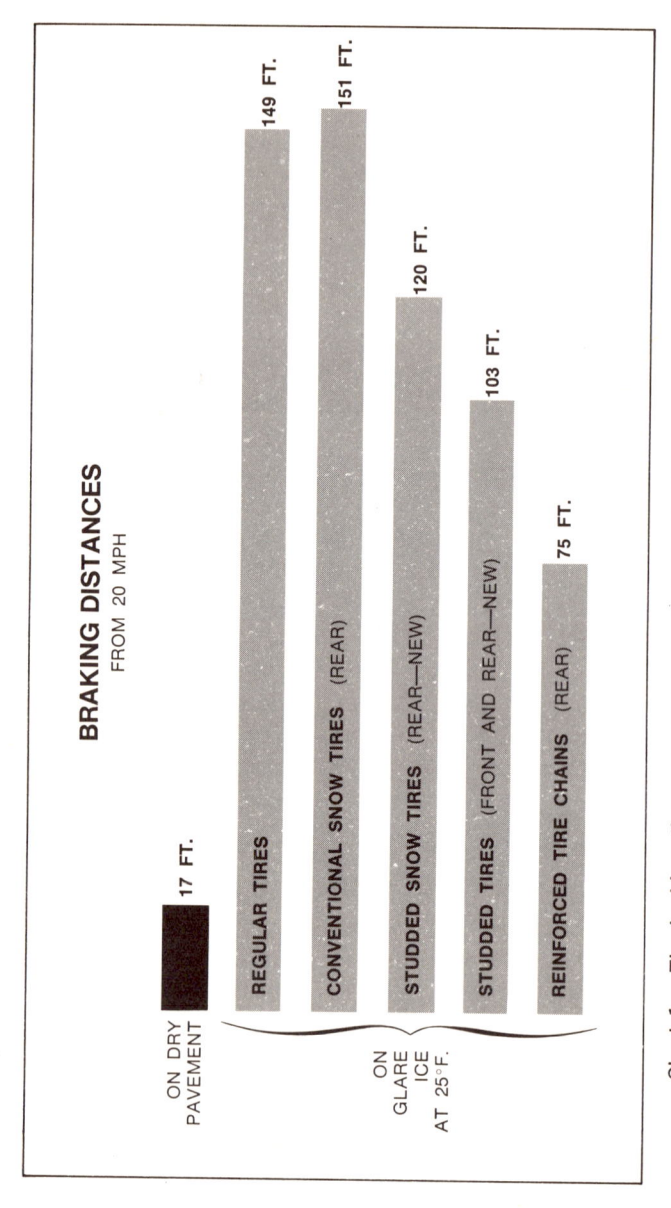

ON GLARE ICE AT 25°F.:
- REGULAR TIRES: 149 FT.
- CONVENTIONAL SNOW TIRES (REAR): 151 FT.
- STUDDED SNOW TIRES (REAR—NEW): 120 FT.
- STUDDED TIRES (FRONT AND REAR—NEW): 103 FT.
- REINFORCED TIRE CHAINS (REAR): 75 FT.

Chart 1. The braking distances shown above do not include reaction time, which normally adds another 22 feet to the braking distances. Also, these figures should not be interpreted as accurate for all conditions.

MINIMUM STOPPING DISTANCES IN FEET

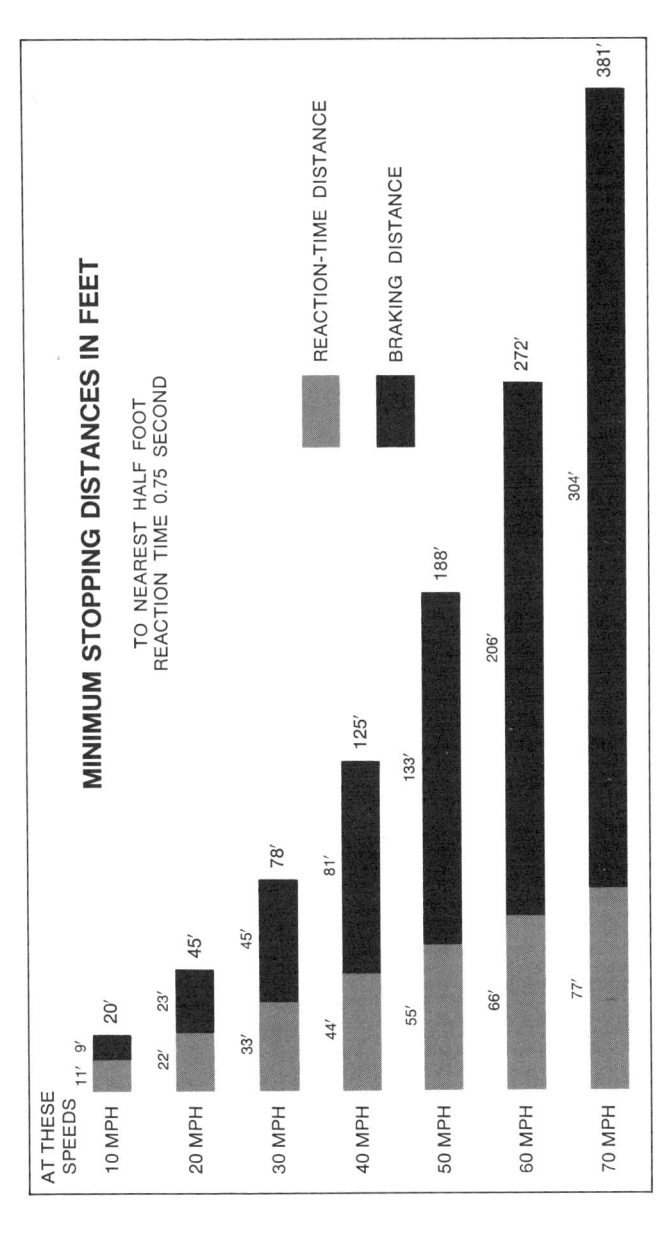

TO NEAREST HALF FOOT
REACTION TIME 0.75 SECOND

AT THESE SPEEDS	REACTION-TIME DISTANCE	BRAKING DISTANCE	TOTAL
10 MPH	11'	9'	20'
20 MPH	22'	23'	45'
30 MPH	33'	45'	78'
40 MPH	44'	81'	125'
50 MPH	55'	133'	188'
60 MPH	66'	206'	272'
70 MPH	77'	304'	381'

Chart 2. Since the stopping distance in any given situation is dependent on such factors as tire condition, road surface and weather conditions, this chart can only show a comparison of hypothetical stopping distances at various speeds.

so all braking must be initiated much sooner than on dry pavement.

If there is a secret to safe winter driving, it is learning to anticipate not only what the other drivers and cars on the road are going to do, but also how your own car may at any moment respond to the road conditions.

Driving on hard-packed snow or sheer ice is a relatively straightforward exercise in restraint and early action. Learn to begin all steering, braking and cornering before they are absolutely necessary and without any erratic changes in the car's speed. Then, carry out these changes with a gentle touch—without jerky motions or heavy-handedness.

The best way to learn the winter-driving "touch" is to practice on a snow-covered parking lot where you can afford to make mistakes without jeopardizing other people or their property. Do all the braking, steering and skidding exercises outlined in the previous chapter, beginning at a very low speed and gradually working up to the point at which you lose control of the car (this will probably also happen at a very low speed).

Go back and do the exercises again and again until you feel entirely relaxed about sliding and skidding and braking and can easily, without panic, make corrections to the car's behavior.

At this point, you will be a far safer winter driver than about 90 percent of the other drivers on the road. And because you have a thorough knowledge of a car's behavior on slippery surfaces, you will be able to anticipate and avoid trouble by watching the behavior of the vehicles and drivers on the road ahead of you.

Considering the possibilities for getting into trouble on snow- and ice-covered roads, surprisingly few motorists actually lose control. This may be because the hazardous road conditions are right out in front of them in plain view, acting as a constant reminder to drive cautiously.

But these same drivers manage to do a lot of unintentional skidding and sliding late in the afternoon of a com-

VEHICLE STOPPING DISTANCE
FROM 45 MPH ON WET PAVEMENT

WET "GOOD" PAVEMENT

NEW TIRES
100 FEET

WORN TIRES
140 FEET

WET "SLIPPERY" PAVEMENT

NEW TIRES
225 FEET

WORN TIRES
450 FEET

Chart 3. How worn is worn? How slippery is slippery? Different tires on different surfaces may produce quite varied results, so this chart should be used for comparison only.

Illustration 9. Climbing a slippery winter hill in a zigzag pattern. When the driver has reached almost the right-hand edge of the road, (A) he turns the steering wheel hard to the left without lifting his foot from the accelerator pedal. (B) The rear end of the car swings to the right, the front end points left and the car heads diagonally up the hill until it reaches the opposite side of the road, (C) where the procedure is repeated again.

paratively warm winter day. When the sun is high during the day, the snow and ice on the road and along its edges melt, forming slush and large puddles on the road surface. Late in the day, the temperature drops below freezing and, in what seems like minutes, the entire road is a sheet of very slick ice.

Winter road conditions are capable of changing so quickly that the only protection against unexpected frozen patches of road is for the driver constantly to monitor the road surface. One of the best ways to check the slickness of the road is to lock up the brakes for a moment. With practice, you will be able accurately to judge the road conditions by the distance your car slides. To stop the slide, merely lift your foot from the brake pedal.

Another way to check for freezing roads is to give a quick jab on the accelerator pedal, noting the ease with which the rear wheels spin. Or, if your car is equipped with manual steering, a sudden reduction in the effort required to turn the steering wheel is a sure sign that the road has turned slippery. So, slow down, drive with a steady but delicate touch, be prepared for a skid at any time and concentrate on squeeze braking.

OFF-ROAD RECOVERY

Most drivers are unaware, until they suddenly hear gravel striking the underside of the car, that their cars have moved off the road surface onto the shoulder. It is easy enough to get into this situation on a two-lane rural road. Just tuning the car radio is often enough diversion of driving concentration to allow the car to drift off the road surface.

If you do not panic, having both right wheels off the road is an easy situation to drive out of. Without braking, allow the car to slow until it is under control, two wheels on the pavement and two wheels off. Now, turn the steer-

A   B

ing SHARPLY to the left—at least a full quarter-turn. As soon as you feel the right front wheel climb onto the road surface, begin steering back onto a straight course down the road.

If you do not turn the wheels sharply enough, the front tire will scrub its sidewall against the edge of the road and be unable to climb up over the road edge. Failing to return to a straight-ahead steering position as soon as the front wheel is on the pavement may cause the car to cross into the opposite traffic lane before it can be straightened out.

The recovery procedure is the same even if all four wheels of your car leave the pavement. The only minor difference is that you begin your straight-ahead steering maneuver as soon as you feel the first (left) front wheel on the road surface.

Illustration 10. Off-road recovery. (A) and (B) When the driver discovers the car has left the road surface, he should slow the car until it is fully under control. (C) He then turns the wheel sharply to the left and (D) as soon as the left wheel is on the pavement, (E) returns the steering wheel to the straight-ahead position so the car will stay in its own lane when it is fully back on the pavement.

TIRE BLOWOUTS

Although tire blowouts are becoming increasingly scarce because modern industrial technology is producing tires stronger than ever before, the blowout is still within the realm of possibility and every driver should know how to deal with it.

In the event of a rear-tire blowout, the rear of the car will swing toward the side of the road on which the tire is located. When this happens, take your foot off the accelerator and countersteer, as you would to correct oversteer or a mild skid. With the car under control, you can pull safely off the road onto the shoulder.

A front-wheel blowout will pull the car to the side of the road on which the blown-out tire is mounted. If, for example, the right front tire blows out, the car will display a strong tendency to steer itself off the road to the right. The driver, in this case, should get his foot off the accelerator, keep it off the brake and steer to the left to maintain directional control of his automobile until it is traveling slowly enough to pull safely onto the shoulder.

LOSS OF BRAKES

Even though the Federal Department of Transportation, since January, 1968, has required all cars to be built with a dual-circuit braking system, your car can still lose its brakes. The government regulation guards against brake loss from a hydraulic leak in the system, but it will not keep you from burning up the brakes while descending a mountain.

When you get to the crest of a hill and are facing a long, steep downgrade, immediately shift to a lower gear. Use the lowest gear available to gain the maximum engine-braking effect and keep your foot off the brake pedal until the car is traveling faster than is comfortable. At that point, brake fairly hard to slow the car to an almost complete stop,

A "blowout simulator" has been developed by GM for their Advanced Driver-Education Program. This device deflates the tire as quickly as an actual blowout, then reinflates it from an onboard compressed air tank while the car is moving.

then ease off the brakes and let the car slowly build up speed again. This gives the brakes maximum time to cool off between exertions.

STAYING AWAKE

Often the most difficult aspect of a long automobile trip is staying awake. Even if you are not physically exhausted and in danger of falling fast asleep at the wheel, there is still the possibility of dozing off from the sheer boredom of miles and miles of fence posts flying past the car's windows.

The only proven cure for sleepiness is sleep. If you are trying to drive a long distance (either during the day or night) without adequate rest and keep feeling sleepy, the safest solution is to pull off the road and sleep for a few hours.

If, on the other hand, you have slept enough to make the trip safely but still have trouble resisting the mesmerism of the highway, you can fight the boredom by stopping every hour and running five circles around the car to get your blood circulating and the kinks out of your muscles.

Or you can play a little game with yourself. Glance in the rear-view mirrors at least once every thirty seconds, which every driver should be doing anyway, and make a mental note of the color and type of each car in view as well as its position in traffic. Then, without looking in the mirrors, try to repeat to yourself where each car is in the pattern. This is not only a good driving practice but a good exercise as well to keep you alert. If a car disappears from the pattern, find it before making lane changes—it may be right next to you.

5
The Accident

THERE IS NO SUCH THING *as an auto accident. There are human errors and mechanical failures and combinations of the two, but fate has little part in the process.*

Every auto accident can be scientifically reconstructed, analyzed and described in the most minute detail. In the majority of the several thousand cases investigated by government and university (multidisciplinary) investigation teams, the conclusions are the same—human or mechanical error, or both.

An auto accident can be reduced to the following four separate stages:

(1) The Potential Accident

(2) The Accident Situation

(3) The Accident or Impact

(4) The Postaccident

These are progressive stages, each one requiring some decision or action from the driver to keep him from going on to the next level.

For example, two cars driving onto opposite ends of a one-lane bridge represent a potential accident. When neither driver slows down, they move into an accident situation, and if at that point neither takes action to avoid it, there will be an impact. The remaining decisions will belong to the rescuers.

This is obviously an overly simplified description of a head-on collision, but it illustrates the decisions facing each motorist at the four stages of the accident. Had either driver made a different decision during the first or second stage, the third and fourth stages might never have occurred.

THE POTENTIAL ACCIDENT

Safely completing any automobile trip without an accident is based to a large extent on the driver's ability to identify and avoid potential accidents before they develop.

The human mind, like a computer, is constantly receiving information (inputs) from the driver's hands, feet, eyes and even his inner ear's sense of equilibrium. In the fraction of a second it takes to sort and identify the inputs, dozens of minor decisions are made, many of them based on information (prior experiences) stored in the mind's memory bank.

In our hypothetical one-lane bridge accident, neither driver's mind flashed a warning as he approached the bridge. Neither mind sorted through its range of experience and came up with the possibility of a one-lane bridge being too narrow for two cars. So, neither driver responded by slowing down to look for another car approaching the bridge from the opposite direction.

This process of identifying the potential accident before it happens is not perfect; poor eyesight (one motor-vehicle department recently reported turning away one-fifth of all

In this simulated highway situation,
students are taught to steer away from obstacles,
not to jam on breaks.

license-renewal applicants because they had substandard vision), intoxication (half of all fatal accidents are thought to involve the use of alcohol), anger, fatigue and stubbornness can all be responsible for the brain never responding to the information the driver's senses are supposed to be reporting.

On the other hand, the circuits may also be overloaded with too much information. With his mind sorting information as fast as the most advanced computer, the driver observing the scene in Illustration 11 must make a split-second decision that accounts for all the variables lying before him. He must consider that

(1) the bicyclist, who is unprotected, will have to swing to the left to avoid the parked truck, and the driver will have to swing to the left to avoid the bicyclist;

(2) there may be stopped cars and crossing pedestrians on the road ahead;

Illustration 11. Driver's view, heavily congested area.

(3) the high-density shopping area to the right indicates potential pedestrian traffic and the opening of car doors into the flow of traffic;

(4) traffic may merge from alleyways, side streets and other blind locations at any moment; and

(5) there are few potential escape routes because of the "hard targets"—lampposts, signposts, buildings and trees—along both sides of the road.

The driver's best solution in this case is to check his mirror for a clear left lane and move into it, minimizing the risk to the cyclist (top priority) and to himself (second priority). This whole computation, from first view to solution, should take as long as it takes to look in the rear-view mirror and turn on the directional signal.

In a sparsely settled area, with fewer inputs for the driver's mind to sort through, it is often easier to decide on a course of action.

Illustration 12. Driver's view, sparsely settled area.

In Illustration 12, the driver must consider that

(1) the pedestrians in the right foreground are probably unaware of the car's approach and therefore cannot be counted on to protect themselves;

(2) the oncoming car eliminates the possibility of swinging a wide left around the pedestrians; and

(3) the blind corner ahead and obscured driveway to the right, at the end of the fence, are unknown quantities and thus pose a threat.

Here, the unprotected pedestrians are the immediate problem. In the split second it takes to observe this scene, the driver must begin braking while keeping almost full concentration on the pedestrians. He can resume speed only after the oncoming car has passed, the pedestrians are behind him and he is able to see into the hidden driveway and around the blind corner.

Even without speed controls, traffic in heavily congested

areas will always tend to move more slowly than in sparsely settled areas. A driver's mind can deal with only so much information in a given time span, so his natural tendency when he feels uncomfortable about his ability to cope with all that is going on around him is to slow down the flow of information reaching him. This means slowing down the speed at which his car is traveling past the information his eyes must scan.

One of the most effective techniques of slowing the speed with which the traffic information must be processed is to allow more distance between your car and those around you. While driving in traffic, concentrate on the distance you are allowing between your auto and those in front, behind and on either side. You will find there is an imaginary zone between your car and those ahead. When it is violated (getting too close to the vehicle in front of you), you begin to feel nervous and have to drive with a very high level of concentration, not in itself dangerous except that a disproportionate amount of your mind is dealing with the possibilities of hitting the car ahead, leaving other possible areas of danger unattended.

Once you find the dimensions of the zone you are most comfortable with (it may be two car lengths and it may be five car lengths, depending on the individual driver), repeat the same exercise with the areas to the left, right and rear of your automobile until you work out the boundaries of an imaginary protective envelope all around you.

The freeway driver in Illustration 13 chose a relatively large protective envelope for himself. If this area were violated, he would have room to move a lane to either the left or right to reestablish a comfortable distance between his car and the others on the road.

From his position within the protective envelope, a driver allows himself time to scan the maximum amount of potential accident information as well as allowing enough physical distance between himself and the other vehicles on the highway to take evasive action should a potential accident develop into an accident situation.

THE ACCIDENT SITUATION

Although every accident contains four distinct phases, it is often difficult to separate the event into its segments while it is taking place. The most difficult distinction to make is that between the potential accident and the accident situation. Many times, a driver will entirely miss the presence of a potential accident, facing instead an accident situation before he knows something is wrong.

The simplest way to understand the difference between the two stages is to remember:

(1) A potential accident is when you *think* you may have an accident if you do not take some kind of action.

(2) An accident situation is when you *know* you will have an accident if you do not act.

Illustration 13.

A

B

C

Illustration 14. Collision avoidance to the outside. (A) The driver of the oncoming car sees just the nose of a car entering from his right, (B) but is not sure whether or not it will stop. By the time it is evident the entering car is not stopping, (C) the driver of the oncoming car is already looking ahead to see if the lane to his left is clear and (D) begins his move into that lane, alongside the entering car and (E) safely past it.

It is the difference between seeing a youngish man step off the curb a hundred yards ahead and seeing in the street directly in front of your car a twenty-year old man with shaggy blond hair, blue eyes and a mole on his chin. The first example calls for an adjustment of your car's speed; the second demands immediate and drastic action.

The single most important element in the transition from potential accident to the accident situation is the driver's thought process. When he sees a potential accident forming ahead, he must begin trying to guess what is going to happen in the next few moments and, based on that projection of events, he must choose his avenue of escape. If the potential accident turns into an accident situation, the driver's mind is already programmed with an avoidance plan and route.

There is no one right or correct escape route that can be used in all situations because there is no standard or uniform accident situation. There are, however, some general guidelines that apply to choosing an escape:

(1) The best escape, if you are not being pressed from behind, is to stop before reaching the immediate scene. Use evasive action only when you cannot stop in time.

(2) Plan a route that will take you out of the path of the accident *and* all the way past the accident scene.

(3) Check both rear-view mirrors to be certain your planned route will not interfere with traffic coming up behind you.

(4) If there is a choice of moving left or right, always steer right, away from oncoming traffic.

THE ACCIDENT

Even with the best planning, it is not always possible to avoid an accident, but that does not mean you have to close your eyes and just let it happen. You may not be able

Illustration 15. Collision avoidance to the inside. (A) With an entering car suddenly directly in his path, and no time to check for a clear escape to his left, (B) the driver of the oncoming car immediately begins moving to his right and (C) safely escapes a collision by tucking into the space left behind the entering car.

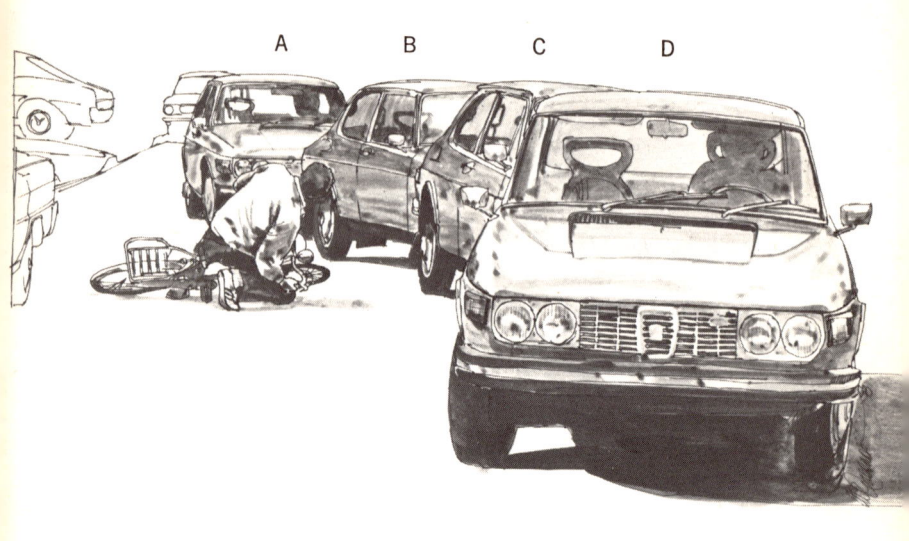

Illustration 16. Pedestrian avoidance to the outside. (A) The driver is suddenly confronted with a fallen bicyclist directly in his path. (B) If he knows the road ahead is clear, he immediately begins evasive action to the left side of the road, (C) getting well clear of the bicyclist (D) before heading back into his own lane.

to avoid an impact, but you still have a choice about *what* you hit.

There are hard objects, like bridge abutments, and soft objects, like roadside bushes. There are objects designed to be hit—for example, guard rails—and objects not designed to be hit—telephone and utility poles. Some trees—small pines and two-inch diameter saplings—bend on impact while others—large oaks and maples—will stand steadfast against almost any automotive assault. The important thing about these various targets is that, in most cases, you can choose which you hit. And that can be the difference between life and death or minor bruises and major injuries.

Illustration 17. Pedestrian avoidance to the inside. (A) When a bicyclist falls directly in his path and (B) the driver knows he cannot steer left because of the oncoming car, he immediately begins steering to his right, away from both the unprotected human being (top priority) and the oncoming car (second priority). (C) He brakes and aims at a parked car, which is the only place he can go. (D) When he is well clear of the bicyclist, he cranks the steering wheel hard to the right to minimize or possibly avoid the impact into the parked car.

Illustration 18. Avoiding a head-on collision. (A) Entering a narrow side road, the driver sees a car coming toward him in the center of the road. (B) He steers as far to the right side of the road as he can, (C) while carefully observing the other car. When it is evident the two cars will collide, (D) he steers hard to the right and aims at the hedge—a soft target—and hits it rather than the other car—a hard target.

This choice between hard and soft targets is not solely limited to inanimate objects. The most crucial decisions are often between the unprotected human (bicyclists and pedestrians) and automotive sheet metal. There should NEVER be any hesitation in this decision. THE FIRST RULE OF SAFE DRIVING IS ALWAYS TO SAVE THE HUMAN LIFE. If this involves driving into a parked car (as the driver did in Illustration 17) to save a human from death or serious injury, you should have no reservations about doing it. Dented and twisted sheet metal can be repaired much more easily than broken bones and torn muscles.

Even in an accident in which all humans are protected by the structure of their cars, the impact they are subjected to can be significantly reduced if the drivers involved do not panic and give up control. It is seldom necessary to hit another vehicle squarely in the front or back, or for your car to be hit squarely. A hard turn of the steering wheel out of the collision course at the very last moment before an impact can often turn a direct hit into a glancing blow.

THE POSTACCIDENT

If you have been able to overcome the initial panic of facing a certain impact, and you have done your best to reduce the injury potential of that impact, turn off the ignition switch to reduce the possibility of a spark-induced fire.

In the immediate aftermath of an impact, the driver (or anyone else physically able) must begin at once to protect those involved from further injury. Because each accident is different, with its own circumstances and complications, there is no set procedure for rescue operations.

There are, however, some specific actions that must be taken in every accident. The number of people available (including other motorists who stop to help) is often the determining factor in the sequence (and speed) in which these things are accomplished. Remember, however, this is a list of all the things that should be done, but not necessarily in the order shown. Every post-accident, just as every accident, is in some way unique, and the rescue attempts must be adapted to the occasion.

(1) Immediately send for police and an ambulance.

(2) Turn on the emergency flasher systems of all cars at the accident scene to warn approaching drivers of the hazard, and place flares on the side of the highway at least 150 yards behind the wreckage. If you are on an undivided road, light another flare the same distance ahead.

(3) Check all cars in the accident for possible fires and search for leaking gasoline. Feel, taste and smell any fluids dripping on the ground to determine whether they are gasoline, oil, transmission fluid, antifreeze or water. Gasoline is the only one flammable enough to be dangerous.

(4) Cover those injured, keep them warm and move them as little as possible until medical help arrives. Move accident victims to a safe place at least 100 yards from the wreckage ONLY if there is a chance of fire.

(5) Question the occupants of any cars involved to make sure no one was ejected onto the road at the moment of impact. Search for those missing and remove them from any area where they might be run over by another car.

When the police and the ambulance crew arrive, stay calm and cooperate in any way you can, but try not to interfere with the job they have to do. Although you think you are being helpful, you may (because you are in shock) only be a detriment to the process.

Half an hour after an accident takes place is not the time to be worrying about insurance, traffic violations or who was at fault. The police are not interested in who you think caused the accident; their job is to fill out an official accident-report form, move the injured to medical facilities and clear the wreckage off the road. There will be plenty of time later to negotiate with the insurance companies involved.

THE SAFE DRIVER

America's reliance on the automobile as the nation's primary mode of transportation has forced almost everyone to drive whether or not he enjoys it. We are taught which pedals to push to make the car go and stop; we practice parallel parking, gear shifting, flat-tire changing; we learn how to read road signs and road maps. These skills are all needed to drive a car, but none has much to do with driving safely.

Safe driving is a combination of self-taught physical and mental skills that equip the motorist to recognize and counteract dangerous conditions before it is too late. There is no way this knowledge can be absorbed through reading a book or listening to a lecture. If you want to be a safe driver, you have to practice both the physical handling skills and the mental thought processes every moment you are operating a car.

The aim of this book has not been to teach *the* way to drive—there is no one way. Our goal has been to outline an analytical approach to driving—from the choice of a basic vehicle and its options to dealing with an accident and its aftermath. We have stressed the decisions facing the driver.

Manual dexterity and a seat-of-the-pants knowledge of how cars handle are important assets for any driver. The ability to think about what is happening on the road and to act decisively and skillfully to stay out of trouble is the key to safe driving.